SACRAMENTO PUBLIC LIBRARY
828 "I" Street
Sacramento, CA   95814
5/10

D1164920

STINGRAYS

A Buddy Book by
Deborah Coldiron

ABDO
Publishing Company

UNDERWATER
WORLD

VISIT US AT
www.abdopublishing.com

Published by ABDO Publishing Company, 8000 West 78th Street, Edina, Minnesota 55439.

Copyright © 2008 by Abdo Consulting Group, Inc. International copyrights reserved in all countries. No part of this book may be reproduced in any form without written permission from the publisher. Buddy Books™ is a trademark and logo of ABDO Publishing Company.

Printed in the United States.

Coordinating Series Editor: Sarah Tieck
Contributing Editor: Michael P. Goecke
Graphic Design: Deborah Coldiron
Cover Photograph: Photos.com
Interior Photographs/Illustrations: Clipart.com (page 11); Brandon Cole Marine Photography (pages 5, 7, 9); Corbis (pages 5, 19, 30); Elasmodiver.com: Andy Murch (page 7); Image Quest 3-D Stock Library and Wildlife Photography: Roger Steene (page 28); Minden Pictures: Kevin Deacon/Auscape (pages 18, 19), Becca Saunders/Auscape (page 25); Mira: David Fleetham (page 13); Photos.com (pages 5, 13, 18, 19, 21, 23); Place Photography: Bruce Farnsworth (page 28); Jeff Rotman Photography (pages 17, 19, 27, 29)

Library of Congress Cataloging-in-Publication Data

Coldiron, Deborah, 1973-
    Stingrays/Deborah Coldiron.
       p. cm.—(Underwater World)
    Includes index.
    ISBN 978-1-59928-817-8
    1. Stingrays—Juvenile literature. I. Title.

QL638.8C65 2007
597.3'5—dc22

2007014856

Table Of Contents

The World Of Stingrays

Every living creature needs water. Some animals not only need water, they live in it, too.

Scientists have found more than 250,000 kinds of plants and animals living underwater. And, they believe there could be up to one million more! The stingray is one animal that lives in this underwater world.

FAST FACTS

Seventy percent of Earth's surface is covered in water. Stingrays make this underwater world their home.

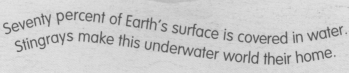

Southern Stingray

Marbled Stingray

Blue-Spotted Stingray

Stingrays are fish with flat bodies and **venomous** tail spines. There are more than 100 kinds of stingrays on Earth.

One of the smallest stingrays is the Atlantic stingray. It is about one foot (30 cm) wide. One of the largest is the smooth stingray. It is about six feet (2 m) wide and 14 feet (4 m) long.

FAST FACTS

Some of the largest stingrays have tail spines more than one foot (30 cm) long!

Smooth Stingray

Atlantic Stingray

Stingrays live in tropical and **temperate** oceans all over the world. A few stingrays are even found in freshwater rivers in South America and Africa.

Stingrays spend most of their time resting on the bottom of a sea or a river. They often burrow in the sand or mud. When they do this, only their eyes and tail are visible. Their flat bodies and skin color make it easy for them to hide!

FAST FACTS

Most stingrays are bottom dwellers. But, pelagic stingrays spend their lives swimming through the open ocean.

It can be hard to see stingrays when they are buried in the sand.

Ready For A Close-Up?

Stingrays have either round or diamond-shaped bodies. Their narrow tails have one or more **venomous** tail spines. Their eyes are located on the top side of their bodies. Their mouth and nostrils are on the bottom side.

FAST FACTS

Stingray tail spines have barbed edges that angle away from the tip. The spines grab and tear as they are removed from wounds.

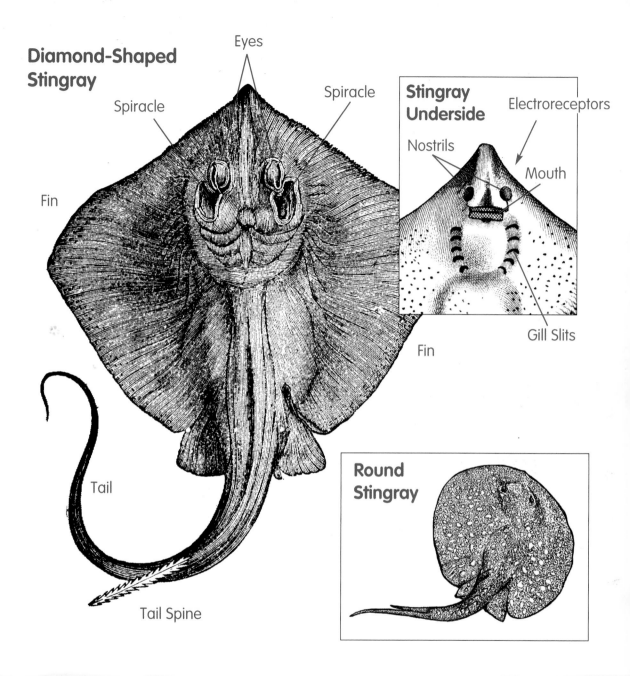

Diamond-Shaped Stingray

Eyes

Spiracle

Spiracle

Fin

Tail

Tail Spine

Stingray Underside

Nostrils

Electroreceptors

Mouth

Gill Slits

Fin

Round Stingray

Like most fish, stingrays use **gills** to breathe. They take oxygen out of water as it passes over their gills.

Most fish take in water through their mouth. Stingrays do this, too. But, they also use two holes on the top of their head. These holes, called spiracles, are located near the stingray's eyes.

Water enters the spiracles. Then, it passes through the **gills** on the bottom side of the stingray's body.

Stingrays in the wild spend a lot of time buried in sand. So, taking in water through their mouths would not be easy. The sand might hurt their gills.

Gill Slits

Spiracle

Spiracles are located right behind each of the stingray's eyes.

Stingrays have unusual bodies. They do not have bones. Instead, their skeletons are made entirely of **cartilage**. This tissue is tough, but flexible.

The stingray's skin is covered in slimy **mucus**. This helps them swim fast. The mucus also protects their skin from harmful **bacteria**.

Stingrays have **electroreceptors** near their mouth. This helps them find food.

FAST FACTS

Cartilage is found in the human ear and nose! It also provides necessary cushion in joints, like our knees!

Cartilage In The Human Nose

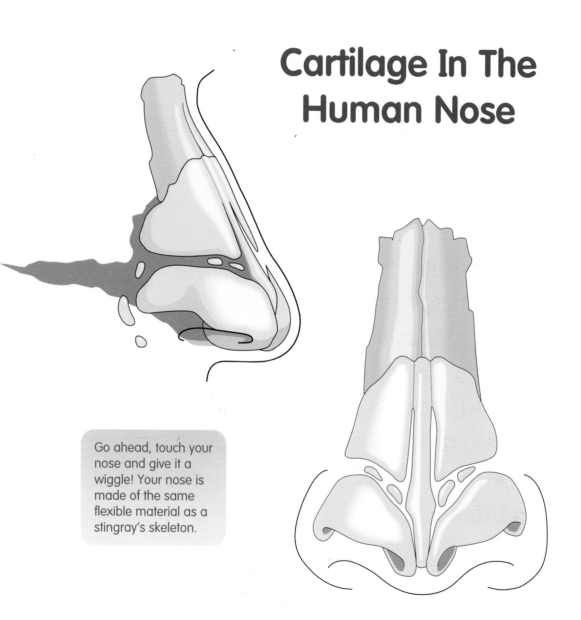

Go ahead, touch your nose and give it a wiggle! Your nose is made of the same flexible material as a stingray's skeleton.

A Growing Stingray

Unlike most fish, stingray mothers do not lay eggs. Instead, stingray eggs hatch inside the mother's body. After the eggs hatch, the babies are born "live." They are called pups.

The amount of time stingray mothers carry their eggs varies from one **species** to another. But, the average is two to four months.

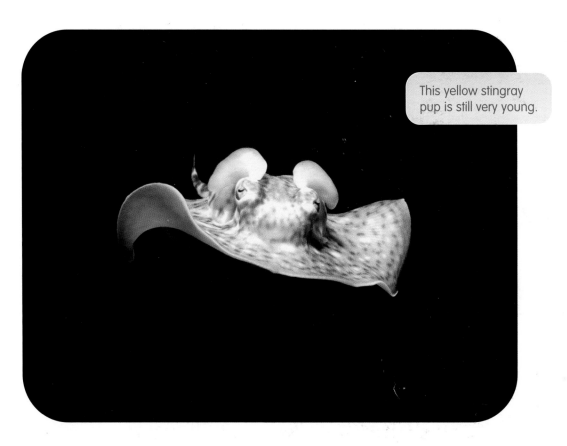

This yellow stingray pup is still very young.

Scientists do not know how long each kind of stingray can live. Each **species** has its own average life span.

Family Ties

Stingrays are just one of many kinds of rays living in our underwater world. Scientists have discovered more than 500 **species** of rays. Other kinds of rays include eagle rays, manta rays, electric rays, and shovelnose rays. Some close relatives include skates, sawfish, and sharks.

Eagle rays "fly" through the water using long tapered fins. They are very good swimmers. Many are even capable of leaping several feet above water! They sometimes travel the open ocean in large groups called schools.

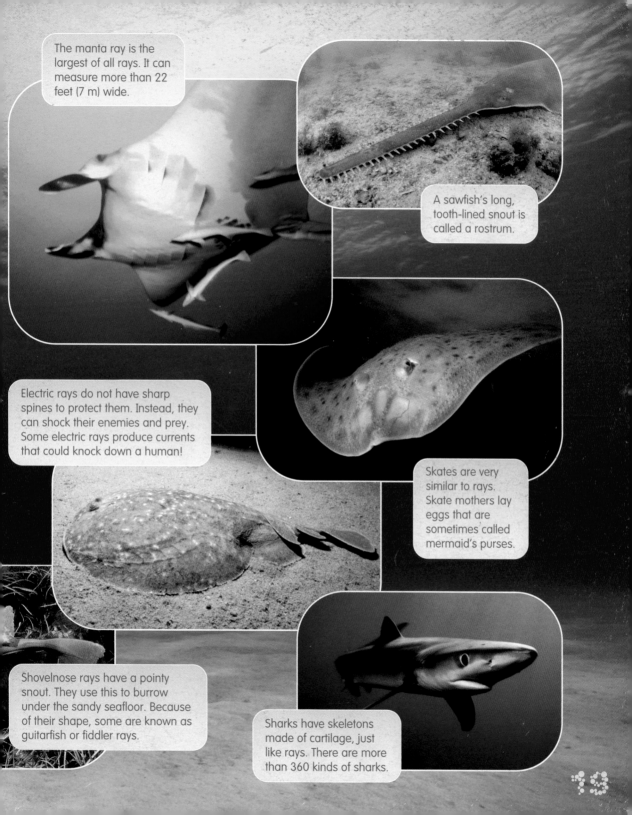

The manta ray is the largest of all rays. It can measure more than 22 feet (7 m) wide.

A sawfish's long, tooth-lined snout is called a rostrum.

Electric rays do not have sharp spines to protect them. Instead, they can shock their enemies and prey. Some electric rays produce currents that could knock down a human!

Skates are very similar to rays. Skate mothers lay eggs that are sometimes called mermaid's purses.

Shovelnose rays have a pointy snout. They use this to burrow under the sandy seafloor. Because of their shape, some are known as guitarfish or fiddler rays.

Sharks have skeletons made of cartilage, just like rays. There are more than 360 kinds of sharks.

A Special Sense

Stingrays feed on **crustaceans** (kruhs-TAY-shuhns) such as crabs and shrimp. They also eat small worms, fish, and **mollusks**, such as clams.

Stingrays have special body parts that help them find food. These are called **electroreceptors**. They are located near the stingray's mouth.

Crabs *(above)*, shrimp *(right)*, and clams *(below)* are among the foods that stingrays eat.

Electroreceptors help stingrays find prey buried in the sand. In fact, stingrays depend on their electroreceptors more than their eyes when hunting.

Electroreceptors sense electrical signals coming from other animals. They let stingrays know how close they are to another animal.

Stingrays have electroreceptors on their undersides near their mouths. The electroreceptors are hard to see. They look like tiny openings in the stingray's skin.

Bath Time

Some stingrays like to visit their neighbors for a bath. Wrasses and Spanish hogfish are two fish that host cleaning stations. These small fish eat harmful **parasites** and **bacteria** found in the stingray's **mucus**. This helps keep the stingray's skin healthy.

FAST FACTS

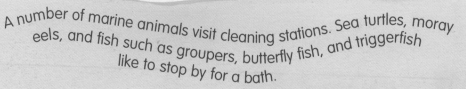

A number of marine animals visit cleaning stations. Sea turtles, moray eels, and fish such as groupers, butterfly fish, and triggerfish like to stop by for a bath.

This triggerfish is being cleaned by a wrasse.

A Dangerous World

Stingrays are well protected by their tail spines. But they do have enemies. They are hunted by large sharks, such as hammerheads and lemon sharks. They are also hunted by killer whales.

Some humans hunt stingrays for food. They also use the stingray's skin to make leather products such as boots and bags.

Stingrays are shy animals. They are not usually dangerous to humans. But, sometimes people step on them when they are hidden in mud or sand. When this happens, the stingray's tail spine can cause a very painful wound.

Stingray tail spines are protected by a layer of skin and mucus. When a stingray stings, the skin is torn and venom is released.

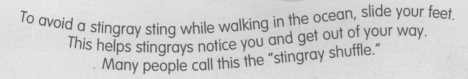
To avoid a stingray sting while walking in the ocean, slide your feet. This helps stingrays notice you and get out of your way. Many people call this the "stingray shuffle."

Fascinating Facts

This mimic octopus is imitating a stingray.

• The mimic octopus has been known to pose as a stingray in order to scare off its enemies.

• The ocellate river stingray lives in some South American rivers. It is more feared by locals than piranhas and electric eels!

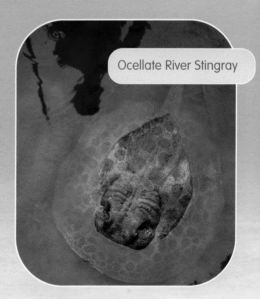

Ocellate River Stingray

Stingray City

👄 The Caymen Islands are home to a popular place called Stingray City. Many years ago, this site was a regular stopping point for fishermen to clean their fish. The stingrays came to eat the fish guts. Today, tourists visit to swim with Atlantic stingrays.

👄 Some people have used stingray tail spines to make spears.

Learn And Explore

Some scientists spend their days studying stingray **mucus**, of all things! Scientists at the Mote Marine Laboratory in Sarasota, Florida, are doing just that.

They want to know why stingrays have such low rates of disease. Their studies may lead to the discovery of new medicines to treat human diseases!

If you are going diving with stingrays, experts say to not wear diving gloves. The fabric can rub off the stingray's mucus, exposing them to bacteria.

IMPORTANT WORDS

bacteria living things that have one cell and can only be seen with a microscope. Some bacteria cause sickness.

cartilage matter that is tough but bendable. A person's ears and nose have cartilage.

crustacean any group of animals with hard shells that live mostly in water. Crabs, lobsters, and shrimp are all crustaceans.

gill an organ that helps underwater animals breathe. It separates oxygen from water.

mollusk an animal with a soft, unsegmented body without a backbone.

mucus a thick, slippery fluid produced by the body for moisture and protection.

parasite an organism that lives on or with a host organism. The parasite benefits from the host in some way.

species living things that are very much alike.

temperate neither very hot or very cold.

venom poison.

WEB SITES

To learn more about stingrays, visit ABDO Publishing Company on the World Wide Web. Web sites about stingrays are featured on our Book Links page. These links are routinely monitored and updated to provide the most current information available.

www.abdopublishing.com

INDEX